SALUTE THE WRECKAGE

Other Books by Clint Margrave

The Early Death of Men, NYQ Books, 2012

Salute the Wreckage

Poems

Clint Margrave

NYQ Books™

The New York Quarterly Foundation, Inc.
New York, New York

NYQ Books™ is an imprint of The New York Quarterly Foundation, Inc.

The New York Quarterly Foundation, Inc.
P. O. Box 2015
Old Chelsea Station
New York, NY 10113

www.nyq.org

First Edition

Set in New Baskerville

Layout by Raymond P. Hammond

Cover Photo by Diliana Stamatova

Library of Congress Control Number: 2016931045

ISBN: 978-1-63045-024-3

Salute the Wreckage

Acknowledgments

Someone recently told me it's easy to become an author, but harder to stay one. I salute Raymond Hammond for allowing me to stay an author and for being a great editor, publisher, and most of all, friend.

I also salute my friends and family who have helped me walk through the wreckage for forty-one years, and the editors of the following journals and presses where many of these poems first appeared:

3AM, American Mustard, The Bastille, Blue Satellite Press, Chiron Review, Cimarron Review, Garbanzo, Ghost Town Literary Magazine, Gutter Eloquence, Kings Estate Press, Misfit, Nerve Cowboy, Pearl, Quincunx (Tangerine Press), *Ragazine, Rappahannock Review, Re)verb, Red Fez, San Pedro Review, Silver Birch Press, So It Goes: The Literary Journal of the Kurt Vonnegut Memorial Library, Spillway, The Teacher's Voice, Turpin's Cave* (Tangerine Press)

Contents

I. Origins

II. Debris Field

III. Alternate Endings

Salute the Wreckage

The wreckage of stars—I built a world from this wreckage.

Friedrich Nietzsche

I. Origins

Origins

Remind me of something forgotten long ago:
Is it the sky that makes the ocean blue or
the ocean that makes the sky blue?
And why on a rainy day do they both look
gray?

If nothing can escape a black hole,
can god? And if he really made the world in
six days
and is perfect and all-knowing
why did it take him so long?
And where did he go?

I don't think the universe bends towards
justice, but I think it ought to.

At eight-years-old I used to stand
in the shower feeling overwhelmed
by the question of existence.

I used to stare at my bedroom wall
just to remind myself I was still looking.

What happened before the Big Bang? Or is it,
what happens before the Big Bang stays
before the Big Bang?

And why does the Dalai Lama wear
a watch? What is time, anyway, to a humble
Buddhist monk?

Who am I? asks the child.
Who was I? asks the grandfather.
Who will I be? asks the college student.

I am one person.
I live on one planet,
orbit one star,
rent one house.

How can E.O. Wilson say ants didn't
change for 110 million years
when I've already changed
fifty times since breakfast?

And what will become of the billions of cells
born inside my body this week?
Will they make me fat?
Or turn into cancer? Or conceit?
Will they make my beard
more white than it already is?

100 billion humans dead
since the birth of our species,
and I'm still mourning
the death of my father.
How many dead dads is that?
Dead lovers? Dead siblings?
Dead friends?

And of the 100s of millions of neurons
targeting my synapses right now, how many
will misfire?
How many will make me sad?

The sky is not blue.
It only appears to be.
And Dawn is just a girl I know.

There never was a chicken before the egg, or
an egg before the chicken.

There never was a first mother
or first father.
A first baseball game.
A first kiss.
A first word.

The first baby
was never born.
The first man never
walked the earth.

Lost

I was ten when my mother left me
at the grocery store.
It must have only been a couple hours.
I didn't take it personally,
spent the time looking for a coin
so I could call her
on the payphone.

Now, thirty years later,
it's she who feels left somewhere,
when she asks me
to pick her up from my sister's house
where she's lived
the past five years.

"I want to go home," she tells me.

"But you are," I insist,
knowing she means back to that place
before old age and dementia
and the death of her husband.

"I am?" she says. "I thought I lived
somewhere else."

It's not likely she'd remember
ever leaving me at the grocery store,
or how when she finally realized it
she called the manager in a panic,
asking if he'd seen a little lost boy
roaming down the aisles,
wondering where
his mother went.

Why Flowers Exist

What used to baffle scientists most
is why flowers exist at all,
how they dominate the earth,
given the energy it takes
a plant to produce them.

Studies put the first flower somewhere
between 140 & 125 million years ago,
sometime before the first romance,
the first apology, the first affair,
the first heartbreak,
the first unwanted pregnancy,
& eventually,
the first poet.

I once refused to buy a girl
flowers for Valentine's Day
because I was so intent
on not being predictable
just to find a bright & heavy
bouquet already in her bedroom
gifted by another man.

And though I knew it then,
I still stayed three more months,
continued to make meaning
out of our relationship
despite having learned
that all flowers

with their elaborate patterns,
colorful petals,
& sweet smelling fragrances
exist only to ensure
that their species' survive,

& all poets are fools.

Family Tree

It was in Missouri,
during the late nineteenth century.

There were three brothers—
my great, great uncles.

One served in the House,
one in the Senate,

the other got hanged for
stealing a horse.

Obligations

"My god," he told all of us,
"I'm the oldest in the family now."

My father was standing in the parking lot
of the mortuary
with my sister Wendy,
my mom, and his two cousins.

Less than a month before his own death,
my great Aunt Pearl,
the last surviving member
of the generation
that raised him,
had died.

Two days earlier,
I received an email
inviting me to her burial:

This is not a family obligation,
he wrote.

Gun Rites

Before there was Newtown or Columbine,
Richard Bourassa shot Jeff Bush.

Before I ever kissed a girl,
he took his stepfather's 12 gauge shotgun
and kissed his best friend.

Before I masturbated or watched my first x-rated movie
he watched blood seep out of the boy's head
and onto the bedroom carpet,
as sirens and parents screamed
through my neighborhood.

Before I snapped (or unsnapped) a bra,
Richard did it again.
This time to lanky, friendless
Christian Wiedepuhl in a dyslexic
game of Russian Roulette.

"My god, am I in trouble for this?"
Richard asked police when he called to report
the second "accidental" shooting
in three years.

Before I could grow facial hair
or get a driver's license.
Before I knew accidents
weren't always accidents,
and losing one's innocence
had nothing to do
with maturity.

My Friend the Christian

Believes when he dies he will go
to heaven and there will be god and Jesus
and angels to welcome him.

My friend believes Adam and Eve
were real people
and that Mary was a real virgin.
My friend himself is a virgin,
waiting for the right Christian girl
who he can marry, saving it all for his
wedding night.

He and I don't talk much about it.
I give him some words of encouragement,
tell him to stick to his feelings,
that remaining a virgin in the 21st century
is more rebellious than being a stud—
even if I don't think Jesus
is a good reason to do it
(or not to).

His other friends make fun of him.
But my friend the Christian
gets in a few jabs of his own,
doesn't act offended
or overly nice in that creepy
sanctimonious tone.

Nor does he hate gay people
or think the godless are going to hell.
I can't imagine my friend the Christian
wanting anybody to end up there.

He knows I think religion is the only
real devil and he doesn't try to save me

or convince me the world is six thousand
years old.

And though we may not ever agree on
the source of charity and compassion,
or where humans come from,
my friend the Christian
and I get along better
than most,

because friendship is secular,
and love is just love.

All My Life

I heard my father
announce himself
to people on the phone.

It didn't matter who,
the pizza man,
the video store,
the phone company.

"This is Tallas Margrave,"
he'd say,
as if the person on the other end
had waited his whole life
for that call.

Lottery

I remember hearing the story
of how my father managed to dodge Vietnam
by first enrolling in college,
then by marrying my mother,
and finally, by having children.

Who could blame him?

I certainly can't, considering
if he hadn't, I might not be here.
Besides, who really wants
to go on a suicide mission
for capitalism?

A home movie from before I was born,
shows my parents and two older sisters
in the mountains,
with smiles on their frozen faces,
necks wrapped up in scarves,
hands covered in mittens
as they build snowmen
in front of a rented log cabin.

Still in their twenties,
my parents would never thaw
to the political heat of their generation's causes,
preferring instead
to kill themselves in the shallow throes
of trying to make a lot of money,

which, if later years were any testament,
after debt and disease
and financial catastrophe,
only proves you can dodge a war
and still be one of its casualties.

Last Night on Nova

An astrophysicist says
there are more stars in the universe
than grains of sand on Earth & I
want to know who's counting?

And though it's approximate
and math people have ways to calculate these things,
it reminds me that I haven't been
to a beach in a while.

Sometimes I get overwhelmed by the life
of the mind, want to be that guy
snoring at the edge of a swimming pool
as UV rays attack my skin.

Sometimes I want to let the shy ones
with no girlfriends figure out the world,
while I drive dangerously
around a mountainside,

drink tequila from a flask
with no lid, smoke cigarettes
like cancer were a winning
lotto ticket.

I want to turn off NPR
& stop obsessing about carbon
emissions or cuts to education,
or who is occupying what.

I want to drink milk
from every genetically modified
hormonally induced
factory farm cow,

stick my hard-earned dollar bills
between some stripper's
in-organic tits,
dump all my trash in the regular bin.

And I want to see the sky
as if it were made for me,
& not worry how many stars there are
or who's counting them.

String Theory

When I
first
learned
to play
guitar
I never
bothered
tuning
because
I couldn't
hear the
difference
between
a guitar
in tune &
a guitar
out of tune
which is
just about
the difference
between
every-
thing.

White

In my parents' house, everything was white.

At birthdays, we ate white cake with white
frosting on white paper plates.
At Christmas, my father strung white lights
on the white flocked tree,
while my mother played Bing Crosby
on an antique white stereo.

The mailbox was as white
as the envelopes inside it.
The telephone as white
as the relatives who called us on it.

There was white carpet in all the bedrooms.
A white couch no one could sit on.
A white piano no one could play.
There was a white television
with shows about the superficial
lives of white rich people.
White chairs at the dinner table.
White napkins on white laps.
White dishes on white placemats.

The kitchen countertop was white
like no meal had ever been prepared on it.
The microwave was white like nothing frozen
had ever been defrosted in it.
The refrigerator, like no perishable item
had ever been kept inside of it.

Every windowsill.
Every cabinet door.
Every bar of soap.
Even the dog was white.

My father smoked white cigarettes with
white filters. My mother leased a white
Mercedes with a white interior.
The white hangers in the closet held white
designer purses, white fur coats, white
brand-named blouses and suits,
all financed on a white credit card
that would forever put them in the red.

No wonder they freaked out
when at fourteen, I dyed my hair black,
wore black nail polish and thick
black eyeliner to school where
white kids called me "faggot"
and threatened to kick my ass,
where fascist skinhead bullies
poured brown syrupy Cokes down my back
in midday lunchtime ceremonies,
and my parents' only concern was
what the neighbors would think,
their only advice that I should
change the way I looked.

No wonder, to this day,
I still refuse to buy any other color,
from my car to my clothes to the pens I write with,
even though I escaped that neighborhood years ago,
their house long sold to someone else,
and the only thing white anymore
is my mother's hair, my father's bones
set in a white wall five years now,
encased in a black box.

Inquisition

I once stood
atop a pyramid in Mexico,
hungover & out of breath,
running away
from my first marriage.
It was the Pyramid of
the Sun or the Pyramid
of the Moon,
I can't remember.

My shirt was drenched
in liquored-sweat,
& I'd already spent the day
examining the ruins,
when I decided to lie down
across the top of the steps
& imagine myself
at an important
ritual bloodletting

to ensure the fate of a crop,
or the prevention
of a future drought,
or maybe as a prisoner of war,
about to be put to
an honorable warrior's death,

except I wasn't a martyr,
& my head hurt,
& all I could think about
was not throwing up

in this place where the Aztecs believed
the universe was created,
where hearts were once

ripped from people's chests,
bodies flung down these same
steep steps, for gods that no longer existed,
by men who no longer believed
in sacrifice.

Paul Gauguin: *D'ou Venons Nous? Que Sommes Nous? Où Allons Nous? (1897)*

> *Gauguin knew his time was running out. He meant this painting to be his last. And so when he finished, he went into the mountains behind Papeete to commit suicide.*
>
> —E.O. Wilson, *The Social Conquest of the Earth*

The baby is not an answer.
The baby is a question.

The couple picking apples is not an answer.
The couple picking apples is a question.

The man with his arms raised is not an answer.
The man with his arms raised is a question.

The statue of a god is not an answer.
The statue of a god is a question.

Don't let the ants take your body, Gauguin.

Suicide is not the answer,
but it *is* the question.

Consolation is imaginary.
You said it yourself.

Let your stone-aged heart relent,
let the mystery of our origins
burn like syphilis,

as you move that vial of arsenic
away from your mouth
and the wastelands
of Paris laugh.

The painting is not an answer.
The painting is a question.

Where Do We Come From?
What Are We?
Where Are We Going?

These mountains cannot hide you.
The brushstrokes call you back.

In His Sleep He Wept

He didn't sleep very long
before he'd jerk up
and look at us.

But when he did sleep,
he wept.

I'd never seen my father weep before
in the way he did
when he was dying.

I'd seen him cry,
but this weeping
came from some other place.

A place no man escapes.

There Must Be Another Way

The smart people say
it's just the way of things:

After four lionesses
surrounded the baby giraffe,
the mother, in one last
desperate act,
charged at them,
kicking out her long legs,
until she lost all balance,
stepping her weight
on top of the calf,
crushing it instantly.

And after realizing
what had happened,
this mammal,
so famous for its silence,
repeatedly opened its mouth
as if trying to scream,
her hooves slipping
on the rocky terrain
when she finally did
try to escape.

And though I know
this is how nature intends
it to be, one creature
preys upon another,
a lion kills a giraffe so
its cubs can feed,
and man, too, has had to
kill in order to breathe,

I will never be smart enough
to accept the agony
on a mother's face
who's trampled her own baby
while trying to save it
from being eaten,
as just the way of things.

Eclipse

The last message came three days
before he died:

"Hello son, can you please
call me back, your mother's
trying to get a hold of you.
Thanks."

I should probably erase it,
instead of having to remember
to resave it every
twenty-one days.

I was teaching a class,
and didn't listen to my phone
until shortly after.

I don't remember much else about that night.
I don't remember any discussions with students,
or what I listened to as I drove home,
or any other messages I might have received.
I don't remember anything except
a total lunar eclipse had made the moon disappear
and I never did call him back.

II. Debris Field

I Never Can

Funny little moon tonight,
my friend says,
I can't make sense of it.

The Arsonist

New Year's Eve and Fred's napkin
catches on a candle
placed at the dinner table
for ambience.

Flames engulf the shriveling cloth
as he holds it up
like a Buddhist monk
observing the impermanence
of everything.

That same night in Hollywood
an arsonist is rolling Molotov cocktails
under people's cars,
and pelting them through
bedroom windows.

I'll read it online before the guests arrive,
note the similarity between
"arsonist" and "artist."

My mind feels more like the former these days,
constantly setting fires I can't put out.

Which is maybe why I don't think *danger*
when the smoke alarm sounds
and Fred dunks his napkin in a glass
of champagne,

and why I constantly
have to remind myself
the purpose of fire is not only
to burn things,

that for hundreds of thousands of years
it's kept man alive
in the harshest winter freeze,
allowed him to boil water
and cook his meat,
brought light into
the darkest caves.

Termino

Driving down Termino, I see the sign
in the upstairs window: *Apartment for Rent.*
"I used to live there," I say to you
before I pull the car over to take a better look.
"I know," you say. "You tell me every
time we drive by." You're not entirely crazy to say
that and I am guilty as charged.

"Don't you want to see inside?" I ask,
getting out of the car before you even have a chance to reply.
I follow the steps up to the front door,
you reluctantly behind me.
"I used to smoke on these stairs,"
I say, peeking through the window
at a living room gutted
except for a lone cable wire,
and some dust balls.

"I even finished my first novel here," I tell you,
reminiscing not so much about the novel
but all the people that passed through the door,
the ghosts of distant friends, the late night
parties and one night stands,
the neighbors always pissed off
and slamming windows.

"Can we go now?" you say, as if you can read my thoughts.
I try the front door, and as predicted, find it unlocked.
The place smells of old cigarettes as our feet creak
across the hardwood floors broken up
by years of termite damage.
I inhale the stale smoke as if it's vintage,
still lingering from some wild party
I had six years ago.

"I always loved the windows," I say,
my voice ricocheting off the walls.
"Over here is where the couch was. And all
my bookshelves were by the door."
"That's great," you say,
"but all I see is an empty space."

And of course it only takes this minor revelation
for me to see it too. All those years living here
falling asleep most nights on the couch alone. All those
parties with people I hardly even knew or liked.
All those friends I gave up for a reason.
Not to mention all those troubled women
and all those cigarettes.

And the termite damage is because the landlord was really
a slumlord who never would fix anything.
And as much as I liked the windows, they wouldn't open,
stuck from years of shitty paint jobs.
And even that first novel
I abandoned shortly after finishing
because it sucked
and no amount of revision
was going to save it.

Just how no amount of revision
is going to save me now
from a past I can't put up for rent
and no longer want to own.

The Necklace

How little a thing is needed for us to be lost or to be saved!

—Guy de Maupassant

I found your necklace
this morning.
It was there, by the bed.
Its fishing wire chain
tracing spheres in the carpet.

Maupassant wrote a cruelly ironic
story about a necklace once,
that turns out to be a fake,
sentencing a young woman
and her husband
to ten years of poverty.

So now, as this ornament
hangs over my hand,
I cannot help
but remember this story,
and how simple the object is
that breeds such a ruinous fate.

Mummies

Once a week I take care of
my recently widowed mother,
the onset of dementia in full effect
after years of suffering from M.S.

We sit in front of the television
at my sister's house, where she now lives,
and at least once a week she says,
"I sure miss your dad."

One afternoon, a commercial
comes on for the Mummies of the World exhibit
at the California Science Center,
showing a 6500-year-old mummified man
and my mother asks,

"Is that what everyone looks like
 when they're dead?"

Seconds later,
realizing there isn't any good answer,
I fumble to change the channel,
but she doesn't
even notice:

She's already falling asleep in her chair,
having wrapped herself up
in a light brown blanket,
preserving what she can.

The Night before He Died

My father yanked out his
oxygen tube,

and asked me what happened
to the sunshine.

The Teller

"Honestly, I thought you were going to rob me," I overheard
the pretty girl at the end of the bar say to her date.

Sunday afternoon and I sat a few stools over
with a couple friends,
waxing nostalgic and complaining
about my fiancée.

"I just thought you were cute," the guy said,
"that's why I slipped you the note."

They couldn't have been much older than 21.

As they took shots and laughed,
the girl moved closer to him.
We all knew where it was headed
and we all rooted for them when they stumbled
out before dark, holding each other up,
giant grins across their faces.

"It's not that I miss being young,"
I said to my friends.
"It's that I miss being happy."

"I miss being young,"
joked my friend Larry.

By the time I got home it *was* dark,
and the violent and jealous woman
I was engaged to marry
threw a wine glass at my face,
just missing so that it shattered against
the front door.

I think it must've only been three weeks later
I wound up at the bank
needing a cashier's check
to pay the deposit on my own apartment
and the same pretty girl
would help me out
for the second time
that month.

Debris Field

Like
that plane on the news,
our love went missing
in the middle of the night.

It gave no distress signal.

Was it a deliberate act
of sabotage?
A suicide mission?
A fire that knocked
out the communications system?

Had a stranger taken over?
A hijacking
with only two hostages?
Sudden and unforeseen
turbulence?

How can something
once so secure,
just crash and burn?

A vast ocean still hides
the wreckage.
A debris field is inevitable.

Meanwhile I listen
for the pings
of that little
black box
I used to call
my heart.

The Road Previously Not Taken

After all the notoriety,
suddenly everyone wanted to take it.
And what started out as a humble dirt path
bending beneath the undergrowth,
had soon been turned into a crowded multi-lane
highway with a carpool lane,
the central artery of a bustling strip mall,
equipped with a Target, a Wendy's,
and even an Apple Store.

The other road that once diverged,
had been bulldozed long ago,
for tract houses and mega churches and a Gymboree,
and the road previously not taken
became run down from masses of travelers causing traffic jams,
leaving broken clumps of asphalt in the streets,
littering it with Target bags,
Java jackets from the newly built Starbucks,
and sticky plastic spoons
from the Frostys they ate.

No longer able to maintain it,
and unwilling to raise any unpopular taxes,
the city neglected the road,
to the point of rendering it *untakeable,*
and despite an eleventh hour attempt
to inject money into making repairs
proved too late to save
the businesses that had folded,
the jobs that had been lost,
the neighborhoods that had been abandoned,
the plywood that had been hammered up across
the windows of all the mega churches.
Too late even to save the Gymboree.

Until ages and ages passed,
and the trees left in the planters
of the abandoned strip mall parking lot
dropped seeds in the cracking asphalt,
and rains washed over everything,
and the winds came,
and new roots began to sprout again,
and the woods grew back,
and after a few more autumns
yellow leaves covered the roofs of all
the abandoned buildings,
and the grasses grew so tall
through the bottom of the rusted shopping carts
that no one could put anything in them,
which made all the difference.

This is Just to Say

I have eaten
the plums
that were in
the icebox

and which
were recalled
from Costco
this week

Forgive me
I am delirious
so sweaty
and so cold

To the Student Who Asked Why He Earned a "C" on an Essay about Love

Because love has its own grammar,
its own sentences,
some that run-on too long,
others just fragments.
It uses a language
not always appropriate
or too informal,
and often lacks clarity.

Love is punctuated all wrong,
changes tenses abruptly,
relies heavily
on the first person,
can be redundant,
awkward,
full of unnecessary repetition.

Every word is compounded.
Every phrase, transitional.

Love doesn't always know the difference
between *lie* and *lay*,
its introductions sometimes
lack a well-developed thesis,
its claims go unfounded,
its ad-hominem attacks
call in question
its authority.

With a style that's inconsistent,
a voice either too critical
or too passive,
love is a rough draft
in constant need of revision,

whose conclusion
rarely gives any sense
of closure,
or reveals the lingering
possibilities of a topic
that always expects high praise,
and more often than not
fails to be anything
but average.

Prelude to a Midlife Crisis

I've started wearing a hat even though
I've been bald for years.

My hangovers last all weekend.

Though I haven't bought the Porsche yet,
I did move to a house that has
a place to park one.

I get annoyed by secondhand smoke.

My blood pressure
seems to be the only thing
that rises.

I suddenly like cats.

My clothes are hip again.

I've had a membership so long
my gym expired.

I drink wine for my health now.

I fall asleep by 10 whether
or not I'm home.

I forget sometimes how old I am.

I forget sometimes *who* I am.

I write a lot of poems like this one.

I think they're good.

Pressed Man

The father died from heat exhaustion.
The car windows had been rolled up,
but somehow the mother managed to escape,
too weak and confused
to rescue him.

In the past, according to the son,
he would leave them at a restaurant
or bring them to work with him,
but just that week his boss had said "no more."

Parents and son had lived together
in his one bedroom apartment.

With nowhere to go
and little aid provided,
Mr. Pressman had left his parents in the car
parked underground
while he went to work
as a bus driver.

I can't help but feel that as
he enters the courtroom
and faces trial for murdering his father,
we are all charged.

You Must Change Your Life

—Rainer Marie Rilke

But what if you like your life?
What if you've finally figured it out?

What if you've found that peace
within yourself or within someone else,
or in the sanctuary
of a quiet neighborhood,
a job that offers benefits,
a reliable car with
a good parking space?

What if, like me, you've moved three times in three years
and don't want to change your life again?

And then there's always the unpacking,
not to mention the circumstances
that drove you to change it
in the first place,
never something good
like you felt inspired
after reading Rilke,

but because you don't
love somebody or they don't
love you anymore
or you can't afford the rent.

There just doesn't seem to be
much choice in the matter.

Change happens
whether you want it to or not,
like getting sick or getting old
or getting audited,

and it doesn't take a poet
to tell you that,

it takes a lifetime.

February 7

A day I can't remember
anyone's birth having occurred,
nobody's death,
nothing that's ever begun
or ended in my life.

Not once do I remember
scheduling an appointment,
starting a new job,
celebrating the anniversary
of something.

Surely somewhere
a mother's now mourning
the loss of her child,
a son is missing his father,
a widow's marking the last time
her husband left home.

Surely somewhere
a license has expired,
a cure is being courted,
a young couple is falling
out of love.

Time Laps

"Especially when your parents were out of *time*,"
a friend from high school
writes in an email,
shortly after my father dies,
reminiscing about the parties
I used to have
whenever they were out of town.

A simple error.

A typographical fumble.

Until it dawns on me
one of my parents
is out of time,

and I don't know
how to reply.

Futile Warning

It's the first thing you notice
as you approach
the Paris catacombs,
asking you to stop
before entering
the kingdom of the dead.

French Phonetics

The absence of a sign is always the sign of an absence.
—Warren Motte

Georges Perec
once wrote
a novel
without
the letter "e"
and called it

La Disparition,

a word
nearly
impossible to translate
in English
meaning

Extinction
or
Disappearance.

But in 1994
Gilbert Adair
found a way
to say
the same
thing
without
putting
back
the
vowel

when
he translated
it as

A Void.

Luck

The jackpot was up to $500 million
and we stopped at the liquor store
to buy a lotto ticket.

I was reminded of a man I read about
in England who hung himself
after playing the same numbers for years,
except the week they hit.

"That's terrible," my ex said.
"There must've been something else wrong."

"If the universe hates you that much," I said,
"what else do you need?"

Later, we checked the numbers
and of course, didn't win anything.

She tore up the ticket
and threw it
in the recycling bin.

"Better luck next time,"
she said,
her words resounding
like an epitaph.

III. Alternate Endings

Revolt of the Books

One day the books revolted
and decided it was time to start banning people.

The first to conspire was *The Catcher in the Rye*
still defensive ever since Mark David Chapman
shot John Lennon.

Then came the Bible, fed up after centuries of being
thrown in the face of others,
cited for every prejudice known to mankind.

Soon, the poems had joined in solidarity.
"Howl," heading up a major picketing event
in front of bookstores across the country.

Even those traitor Kindles agreed to shut down.

People were just too obscene, the books argued.
And someone had to protect them
from their readers.

But like so many other causes what started out
as a peaceful revolt soon turned into a violent one
spearheaded by *Mein Kampf,*

which suggested piling people up
like old Beatles records
and dousing them with kerosene.

And the books realized they'd become
everything they hated and went back on their shelves

dedicated to a future of educating others
about the dangers
of banning people

who had, after all, made them what they were:

Not only filling them with all that hatred and obscenity
but also all that wonder
and compassion

the same people
who had filled them full of love.

The Next War

U.S. Weighs Response to Sony Cyberattack,
With North Korea Confrontation Possible
  —*New York Times,* December 18, 2014

Let the next war be digital.

Let cyber arsenal fall on cyber
infrastructure. Cyber soldiers
secure cyber borders.
Cyber prisoners be
cyber tortured.

Let cyber allies confront
cyber enemies.
Cyber capitalists fight
cyber terrorists.

Let there be cyber protests
on cyber streets.
Cyber debates in
a cyber Congress.

Let our fears be cyber.
Our victories cyber too.

As cyber wives
become cyber widows,
and cyber children,
cyber orphans.

Let blood be digital.

And the hands
that wipe our eyes,
and our mouths
that fill with dirt,
and the flags that drape
our coffins.

Commando

Dad made the final journey without underwear.
None of us remembered to bring any.
We all found it rather humorous,
while making funeral arrangements,
to think of him going to his eternal resting place commando.

"I wouldn't want to be buried in a bra," my sister said.
Even Mom was laughing.
The only one who didn't find it funny
was the funeral coordinator, who, despite her career choice,
seemed shocked by the absurdity.

The Hope Chapel

It's no surprise
that in a mortuary
the Hope Chapel
would be the smallest
and cheapest room available.

Quantum Entanglement

This isn't love
it's quantum entanglement.

I pound a fist in Long Beach,
you feel your desk shake in downtown L.A.
Somewhere in Beijing, a pen drops
from a table as the letter "H" pops off
a computer keyboard in Chicago.

A coin flipped in Amsterdam
lands heads in Zimbabwe.
I set this notebook down
on the kitchen table, and a Russian
bureaucrat feels a cramp
in his left hand.

Outside it's wet,
the rain taps the concrete,
as pigeon shit splatters
a wicker chair in France.

Somewhere on a rooftop in Brooklyn
a girl stubs out a cigarette
and I jolt awake from my nap.

It's four in the afternoon
and you're on a train headed
back to Long Beach,
while I've been asleep
on this couch,
the ground beneath me
rumbling.

What Ahab Needed

What Ahab needed
was a little mindful meditation,
a hot yoga class,
a Swedish massage,
something to unlock his anxious brain,
set him back in the present,
guide him in from the shore,
tell him his thoughts were just thoughts,
a quick Google search
to reveal he wasn't alone.

The Pequod had no benefits package,
& there was no Obamacare
no PPOs, or HMOs,
no disability or Medicare
for a peg-legged man his age,
no diagnosis of
Post-traumatic Stress Disorder.
The birth of Freud was still
five years away,
& the idea of a support group
or self-help book,
wouldn't arrive for
another century.

What Ahab needed
was a little cognitive behavioral therapy,
some "emotional intelligence,"
a good hobby to take his mind off his woe,
a drunken night out with friends,
a tennis racket,
some self-hypnosis relaxation techniques,
a membership to LA Fitness
where he could run in place
and watch TV.

And who hasn't felt themselves
the prey of the universe?
Who hasn't obsessed over the pain,
anger, despair, frustration,
cruelty of existence?
Who hasn't wanted to plunge
their harpoon into the surface
of the mind's sea?

Maybe what Ahab needed
is what we all need:

the wisdom to tell ourselves
that sometimes
a whale is just a whale,
& the best narratives
aren't always the ones
we want to read.

The Death of a Comet

In memory of Christopher Hitchens
April 13, 1949–December 15, 2011

Astronomers predicted the comet
would die inside the sun's corona.
Satellite instruments prepared
to document it for posterity.
Systems tracked it.
Data was collected.

The closer it got, the more
anticipation mounted
as the object's sludgy white tail
began to shed and vanish.

Then something miraculous happened.

The comet, flaring as it dove,
reemerged an hour later,
almost as bright as before,
and in a matter of days,
its singed tail had all but
grown back again.

And though we may not be as lucky,
I cannot help but think
the best of us are like that comet
defying them all
by plunging straight
into the hottest surface,
and living on.

Revising a Letter Already Sent

There's no point in doing it.
Yet I do it anyway.
Take out a word here,
change a verb,
switch the tense
from past to present.

The letter was probably of no importance
to the man I sent it to,
he was dying,
and may or may not
have received it.

Who was I to waste the last
minutes of his life
with bad syntax,
clumsy verbs,
a few awkward phrases?

Was my letter too somber? Too serious?
Too condoning? Too humorous?

Such attempts I make to rewrite
the past, make-up,
rearrange, re-interpret,
revise, re-open
the file.

When all time has a stamp.
Dropped off in a box somewhere.
No chance of getting it back.

Reversal

In a dream I have,
my father's
the one that drives away,
leaving the rest of us
in the cemetery.

Don Quixote

It's hard to fathom
when I began reading
the book, my father
had been alive.

The novel became a refuge for me,
when I finally picked it up
again nearly two months
after he died.

I found myself healing
from Cervantes's magic.

Quixote was alive,
and I was a knight errant,
faithful to the imagination.

I never stopped feeling it.

For months, it was my therapy.
Life wasn't what it was,
but what it should be.

His foolishness, my wisdom.
His madness, my own.
Quixote made the fantasy world real.

And the real world a fantasy.

Death by Ink Eraser

In memory of George Spencer,
February 15, 1894–February 15, 1909

It might have been the worst case of reverse sexual
harassment ever recorded.

Poor George Spencer, dead at 15,
fell on an ink eraser in his own coat pocket
evading birthday kisses
from six female co-workers.

The headline of the 1909 *New York Times*
article the next morning read,
"Stabbed to Death in Office Frolic."

I suppose having your heart penetrated
by a sharp metal object
used to remove ink
while fleeing six smitten women
is still better than
dying on a battlefield,
or facing a firing squad,
or getting cancer.

But at 15, young George learned the hard way
what it's taken me years to figure out:

There are just as many ways to flee
the heart as there are to
penetrate it. And just as much
danger in doing so.

The Knife

When my ex moved out,
she left me one knife.
Other things we divided
more evenly.

For instance, I found one tennis
racket in the closet,
a half loaf of bread
in the kitchen cupboard,
six eggs in the fridge.

She was generous
enough to leave
some wine glasses.
And a few pots and pans.

But she took the scissors
from all the drawers.
The lightbulbs from
all the lamps.

She took the stereo.
And the trashcans.
And the blinds from
the windows.

She took the calendar
and the clocks.
The sheets and all the pillows.
And the bed.

Of course, none of this is true.

It began that way.
With one knife.

And one ex.
And one man,

trying to figure out
why it's so much easier
to make
something up,

than let
something go.

My Love Life and the World Cup: A Recent History

In 2002, I lost all my matches,
was put in a tough group
with Abby, fresh out
of a long term relationship,
Lauren who lived with her boyfriend,
and Bridget who turned out to be schizophrenic.

In 2006, it was an artist named Stephanie,
who tried to take herself out
of the game only months
before our match,
had scars on her wrists
to prove it. Mostly, she just
kicked the ball down
the field and I chased after
it, until one day they carried
me off on a stretcher.

That same year I made it to the semi-finals
with Renee, a bad drunk
who got a red card
after faking too many injuries
and falling on the turf
too often.

Then in 2010, I thought I'd
met my match with Jane,
until we kept competing even
during off season,
always playing defense
so neither one of us
could score,
our fate decided
by our penalties.

Now, it's 2014, and after
a few friendly scrimmages
I wonder how I even like this sport
and why I'm still standing
in the stadium.

The Language of Airports

is the language of life.
All those delays and cancellations.
The take-offs and landings.
Customs and security measures.
Baggage claimed or left unattended.
The layovers. Missed connections.
The recharging stations.
The fueling and refueling.
The control towers.
The fear of mid-air collisions.
Always leaving someone
or something behind.
The long and short flights.
Arriving at your terminal
earlier than expected,
or at the gate standing by,
waiting to depart.

Contact

In today's paper,
I read an article on the SETI project
headed up by Jill Tarter
the woman on whom
Carl Sagan based his novel *Contact.*

When we had begun
to pack up my parents' house
and I was deciding what to take of my father's,
the first thing I grabbed was his collection
of Carl Sagan's *Cosmos* DVDs,
which I remembered watching on television
with him as a child.

There was also the DVD for
the movie version of *Contact,*
as well as Sagan's last book,
Billions and Billions,
which I had given him
for his birthday one year.

That very first Saturday
after he died, I stayed in bed
and watched *Contact,*
which in one scene
describes a meeting with an extraterrestrial
disguised as the main character's
dead dad.

Later in the article,
the journalist quotes Sagan
on his impetus
to write that scene,
saying,

"I always wanted to have
one more conversation
with my father."

Stellar Outcasts

I've read there are stars
that don't belong to any galaxy,
ejected from their homes,
drifting free in the blackness of space.

And there are planets too,
gone rogue, nomads
orbiting the interstellar
deserts of the Milky Way.

I've even heard some talk
intelligent life could thrive
in such a place, if a planet were
to generate its own heat,

long enough for an advanced
species to evolve
knowing nothing of sunrise
or sunset, or photosynthesis.

And though I don't know
any people who have
left their planet yet (not literally
at least) I suppose
we could be the first,

away from the spectrum of primary colors
or the warmth of spring,
away from the dumb
demands of day,

just tourists of the dark.

Sing at Unnatural Hours in the Presence of Artificial Light

There are times I have to remind myself
that a bridge is a way to travel over water
not a diving board for suicides. That airports

aren't just places for departures, but places
for arrivals, and hospitals aren't only
where we go to die, but where we're born.

I'd like to think not a single bomb
was dropped on anyone today, not a single
person was diagnosed with cancer.

Somewhere someone misses you.
A friend remembers something
you once said. Somewhere someone

thinks you're beautiful. A man holds
a guitar in his hands. A couple dances behind
the living room couch mouthing words

they've longed to share with each other.
At this hour only astronomers
and insomniacs find natural,

as the blazing red lights of an ambulance
flicker fear past the window,
I have to remind myself:

it doesn't always mean somebody's
dying in there, sometimes it means
somebody's being saved.

At 72

He never calls us anymore.
He doesn't come home for the holidays,
doesn't see my mother though she misses him.
Sometimes I wonder where he went.
We all do. Because at 72, my father doesn't
know his grandchildren. He doesn't have
a cell phone or email address or Facebook
account. You can't write on his wall or send
him text messages. A Google search reveals
no results. Sometimes, my sister says she talks
to him. Just this afternoon she calls to tell me
she went and visited him for his birthday.
I don't bother asking how he's doing.
Nor do I bother seeing my father at 72.
The last time I tried he was so quiet I could hear
a bird's wings flapping in the sky above my
head. Strangers surrounded him. The whole thing
was really awkward. Since then, I haven't
been back. I suppose that makes me a bad
son. I guess it might be easier to hold a grudge
against him or blame it on my upbringing.
Or maybe just try to accept that at 72,
my father isn't interested in talking to anybody.
He's already been dead for five years.

Alternate Endings

When your sister told you to put socks on your
hands so the monkey bars wouldn't
hurt them, you didn't listen and never
fell and broke your wrist. The night at the mall
when those skinheads kicked your ass,
you at least tried to hit one of them back.
You never smoked a cigarette. And as a freshman
in high school when you saw Jane's Addiction
with those senior Goth chicks whose names you forget,
you never sat a space apart from them
and they never teased you for it. You went
to The Cure concert and not your junior prom.
You saw the car coming before you made
the left turn. Instead of throwing your crutches
at that taxi driver, you asked him for a ride home.
You never married a woman you didn't know,
and never wasted Paris on an ex-girlfriend.
The night you got your DUI you let Dennis drive.
And in the hospital, when your father
was dying, you demanded they move him
to intensive care. Instead of saying no,
you agreed to an autopsy and spared
you, your mother, and your sisters
five years of wanting to know. You went
and saw a therapist before you ever
had a meltdown. Every decision you've
made has been sensible. Your life
is perfect and boring. You never
even wrote this poem.

About the Author

Clint Margrave lives in Los Angeles, CA.

www.ingramcontent.com/pod-product-compliance
Lightning Source LLC
LaVergne TN
LVHW091229080426
835509LV00009B/1215